Hongry Catch the Foolish Boy

*To my father and mother
who also loved to listen to the African storytellers.*

Hongry
Catch the Foolish Boy

By LORENZ GRAHAM
Pictures by James Brown, Jr.

THOMAS Y. CROWELL COMPANY • NEW YORK

By the Author

David He No Fear
Every Man Heart Lay Down
God Wash the World and Start Again
Hongry Catch the Foolish Boy
A Road down in the Sea

L.C. Card 77-184981

ISBN 0-690-40111-6

0-690-40112-4(LB)

1 2 3 4 5 6 7 8 9 10

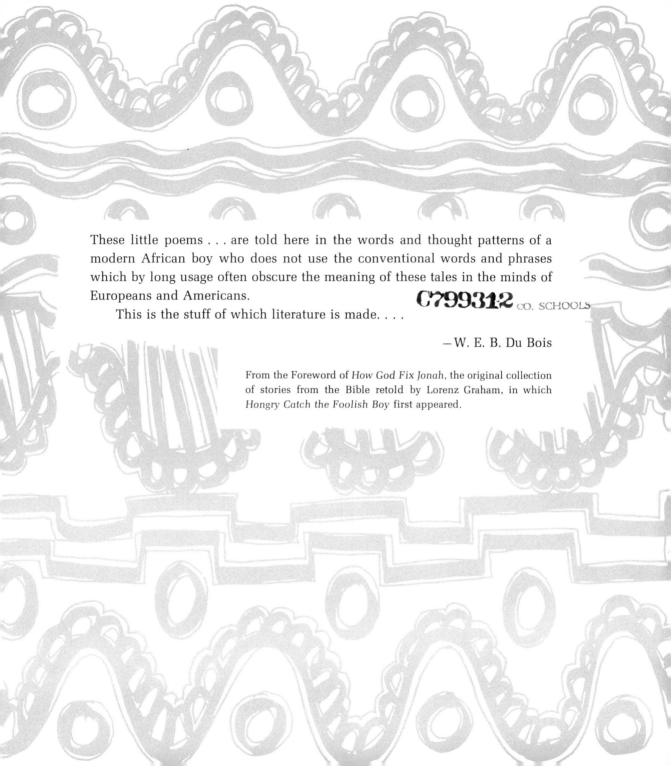

These little poems . . . are told here in the words and thought patterns of a modern African boy who does not use the conventional words and phrases which by long usage often obscure the meaning of these tales in the minds of Europeans and Americans.

This is the stuff of which literature is made. . . .

— W. E. B. Du Bois

From the Foreword of *How God Fix Jonah*, the original collection of stories from the Bible retold by Lorenz Graham, in which *Hongry Catch the Foolish Boy* first appeared.

Introduction

The familiar Bible stories of kings and slaves, of strength and weakness, of love and hate were brought to Africa by missionaries. As they were retold by Africans, they took on the imagery of the people. Shepherd David with his harp of many strings, strong man Samson who was weak for woman palaver, and baby Jesus born in the place where cattle sleep, are now part of the folklore of the country. To the African storyteller the Bible tale becomes a poem, or rather a spoken song. His words are simple and rhythmic. The song is sung, and it is sweet.

It was in Liberia that I first heard many of these tales, recounted in the idiom of Africans newly come to English speech. They can be heard in many other parts of the continent as well — in the west and even in the east, wherever the English settlers spread their language.

Words of Spanish and Portuguese still remain on the African coast. *Palaver* now means something more than *palabra*, or "word." It can mean business or discussion or trouble. When "war palaver catch the country," people must fight, and some must die; and "woman palaver" often lands a man in jail. *Pican*, for baby or son or child, comes from *pequeño* ("small") and *nino* ("child"). The two words flowed together in English speech to become first *picaninny* and then *pican*.

Read again an old story. Behold a new vision with sharper images. Sway with the rhythm of the storyteller. Feel the beat of the drums.

Long time past
Before you papa live
Before him papa live
Before him pa's papa live—

Long time past
Before them big tree live
Before them big tree's papa live—
That time God live.

They be one man what have two sons.
The young son go fore him pa face and he say,
"Pa, make it you give me that part what belong me."
The old man do so.

The young man take up them thing what belong him
And he go.
He go in country where people ain't know him.
He go in country where people ain't know him pa.
The people see him come
The people say
    "Oh!
    He got plenty fine cloth
    He got plenty gold bangles
    He got plenty money
    He be big man for true-true."

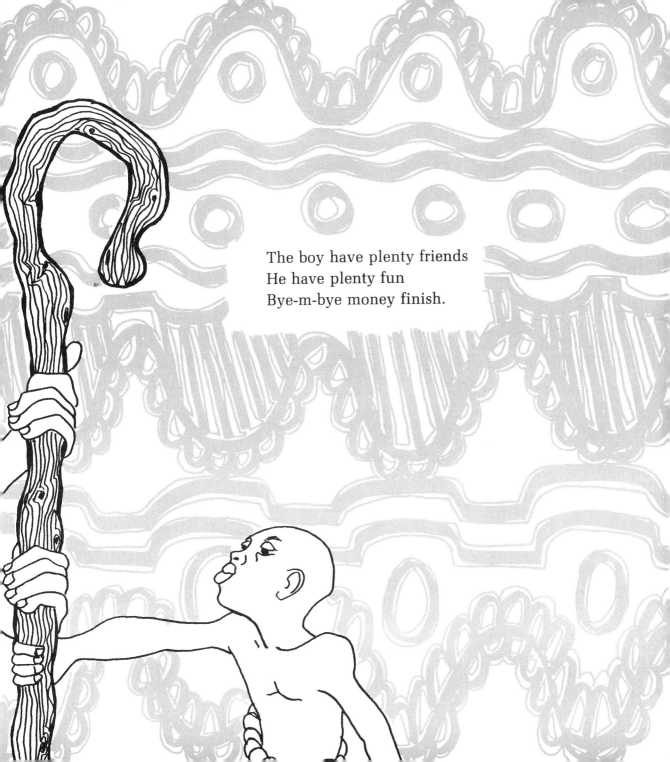

The boy have plenty friends
He have plenty fun
Bye-m-bye money finish.

He look about.
Them people live for friends, no live again.
Then hongry time come on the country
He no got house
He no got chop.
He go fore Mandingo man for beg small chop.
Mandingo man send him in field to mind hogs.

He be poor boy now.
He want fight hogs to eat hog chop.

He sit down. He think.
He think good for him head.
Bye-m-bye he hear somebody say
"How many people work for you pa?"
He say "Plenty."

He think again
And he hear somebody say
"The people what work for you pa,
Do hongry catch them people?"
He say "No."

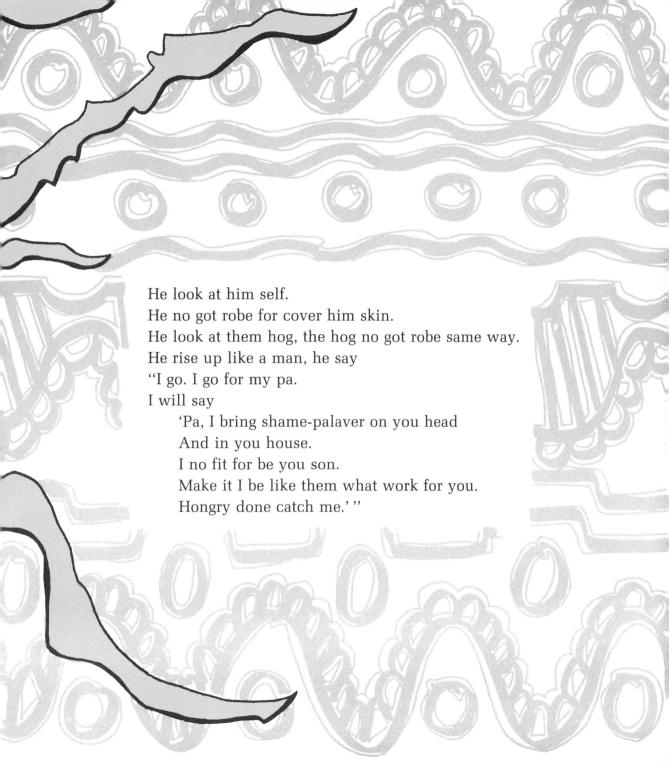

He look at him self.
He no got robe for cover him skin.
He look at them hog, the hog no got robe same way.
He rise up like a man, he say
"I go. I go for my pa.
I will say
    'Pa, I bring shame-palaver on you head
    And in you house.
    I no fit for be you son.
    Make it I be like them what work for you.
    Hongry done catch me.' "

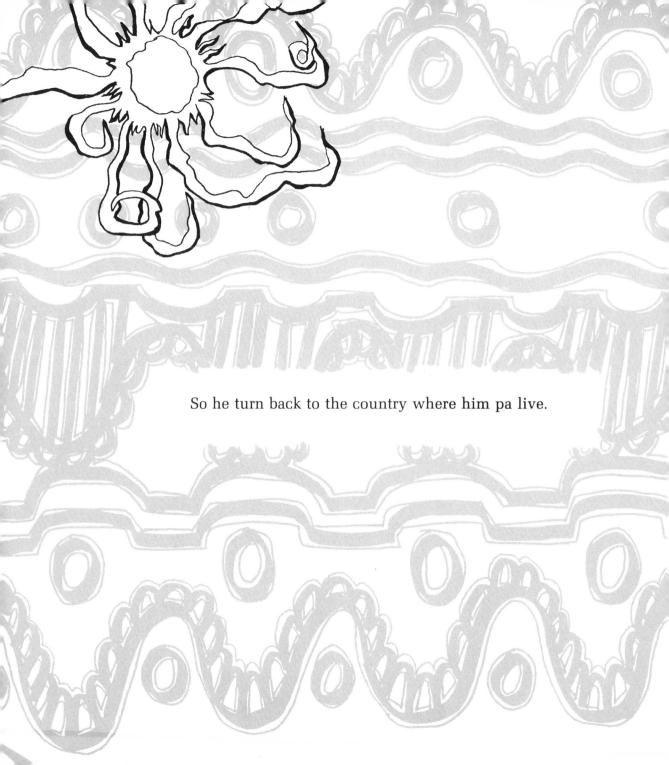

So he turn back to the country where him pa live.

When the old man look up and see the boy come
Him heart turn over.
He run like small boy
He hold him son tight
He kiss him.

The boy cry. He say
   "Pa, I bring shame-palaver on you head
   And in you house.
   I no fit for be you son again.
   I come cause hongry catch me."

But the old man call the people and he say
    "Bring the best robe and put it on him
    Bring gold ring for him finger
    Bring shoes for him foots.
    Kill cow. Kill chicken. Kill goat.
    We going eat meat and drink palm wine
    We going make music, we going dance.
    My pican was dead and now he live.
    My pican was lost and now he found."

Now the first-born son,
He work hard in the rice farm that day.
The sun be plenty hot
The sweat run down.
While he work he hear the drums,
He come see what the palaver be.
The people say
    "You brother done come.
    The old man happy too much.
    He done kill that fat cow.
    He say all people must come for make play."

The boy vex.
He no want make play.
He tell him pa
    "How you do me so?
    All of this time I sit down by you hand,
    I work, I work, I work, I never left you.
    All of this time you never kill
    One small goat for me.
    How you do me so?
    That one bring shame on you head
    But when he come you be happy,
    You make feast for him."

The old man come close.
He put him hand on him boy's head.
He cry small and he say
 "For true,
 You be my pican what make my heart lay down.
 You be my first-born son.
 All the thing belong me, belong you same way.
 But see you brother,
 He was dead and now he live.
 He ain't got nothin
 And he hongry."

The first-born say
"Old man,
I come."

About the Author

Lorenz Graham was born in New Orleans, Louisiana. His father was a minister, and his childhood was spent in a succession of different parsonages. After graduation from high school in Seattle, Washington, the author attended the University of California in Los Angeles. In his third year, however, he left college to become a teacher at a mission school in Africa.

The great disparity between the American idea of Africa and the reality of African life first prompted Mr. Graham's interest in writing for young people. On his return to the United States, the author was graduated from Virginia Union University, and he later did postgraduate work at the New York School for Social Work and at New York University.

Lorenz Graham likes working directly with people and their problems. He has been a social worker and a probation officer. Most of his time is now given over to his writing.

While in Africa, Mr. Graham met his wife, who was also a teacher. They make their home in southern California.

About the Artist

James Brown, Jr., found HONGRY CATCH THE FOOLISH BOY an especially gratifying book to illustrate because, as he says, when he was a child "in my little world, black illustration did not exist." Mr. Brown was born in New York City and studied at the Art Students League and the School of Visual Arts.